CONTENTS

LIFE

LOVE

HEARTBREAK

PERSONAL

A Collection of Poetry

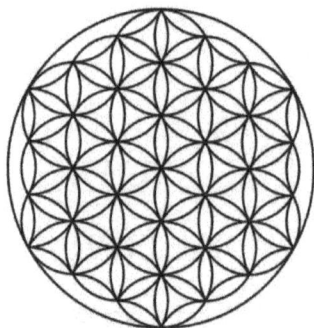

LIFE

Life gets you carried away, carried into a new day
Carried into some bad ways, the only way to survive
Is to play like you don't care, play like your blind
While other people stare, stuck in a world full of confusion
Then you take a step back, and it's a world of conclusion
A world where here is what's right, here is what's wrong
Your mind and your thoughts all live in a stone
Life isn't always what you make it
It can be about what you own, about the riches, the dope
The ones with the finest clothes
The ones who can buy power
All of them have the control, and the ones who don't
Are left behind to build their own throne

Dreams and memories

All live in the same place

Life's a blessing with plenty mistakes

A positive life is what I aim for

Day to day

The world needs more love

More patience more hugs

More understanding of individuality

Comprehending the power of unity

Respecting that it is not only your appearance

But your mentality

Life behind my eyes
Is something sweet
Life behind my eyes
Blessings on repeat
Giving thanks
Straight gratitude
Learn to love what you have
Before it's taken from you
How can you ask for more?
When you are not thankful
For what's in front of you

To be happy with yourself

Is to be happy with your worth

But also, your struggle and hurt

It's to grow

It's to breathe

It's to notice that you're not perfect

And neither are we

Once you're happy you'll know

Because once you're happy you won't let go

Time and time again

I wish for better days

Days that would leave me

Not believing I'm awake

Leave me breathless and stress less

But most of all happy to see those days

Your negativity will not detain me

Because I will not let it

Try and knock me down

Shit will get reckless

I will not fall without a fight

Because I learned giving up

Just isn't a part of my life

Push me push me

You just make me stronger

I'll let you in on a secret

I've made it through some stormy weather

But I am my only fear

And the strength that puts in me

No women or man can diminish my dear

I guess I've been thinking about it wrong

Always wanting to relive the past

Wanting to get it back

But that's the problem

The past should stay behind me

The good in it will remain great memories

Because that's all they can be

No matter how bad I want them back

At least they will always be a part of me

Alone again, my heart cried

What to do when you're stuck inside

Inside where demons lie

They're not my friends

Just dressed in disguise

Where are you going?

Please don't leave me alone

Because once I'm alone

The demons come back home

Living in a world where it's normal to die young
Living in a world where people have to bite their tongue
Where having a gun at 15 is how you show you're "real"
People beating people with bats is how they cut their deals
Shots fired at night but it's all just life
Trying to grow and leave
But all you ever seen was how to bust pipes
All you ever seen was how to hustle to meet your needs
Trying to talk to god and interrupted by the devil
Tell him go away
Because you're praying to go to heaven
In a world like this you have to watch what you say
In a world like this it's less talk more gun play

Is it bad to care what people think?
Is it true that we should all be the same?
Life hurts us in many ways
In good or bad there will always be pain
Learn from it, Grow from it
Don't be ashamed

Happiness is what my heart craves

True, honest, happiness

You and I need to practice this

I want to wake up and be able to smile with no doubt in it

I wish I could ask you to teach me how to stop doubting us

But it's like taking lessons

From a boy who still hasn't found his happiness

Dwelling, Dwelling, Dwelling

Dwelling on the past

Trying to get it back

But it can never come back

Even if it had

It would not be what we had

Think bigger

Instead of wanting something in the past

Create a future you dream to have

Don't let the money consume you

Trying to run it up

Don't lose focus of the true you

Money can only fulfill limited wishes

No matter where you go

What you have

Or what you do

The money will never be you

You are worth way more than gold

You will learn to hold yourself

Above it all

And when you do

Is when you will be the true you

Who are you?

To tell anyone what normal is

A normal family

A normal life

Fuck the word normal

It will not survive

Not in my world

The world filled with

Truth and real

Where your beauty spills

From the inside out

And is never categorized

Or sustained

By stereotypes or people with little brains

Don't judge me

You can't even walk

In your own shoes

In life you will want more
Than what you already have
No matter what place you're in
You will always seek more
Being a human being
This is what you will endure

I never knew happiness could run out

Until I gave all of it away

I want things to be better
So, I must make things better

I was once drowning
Until I finally lift my head up
And realized I was the one
Holding my head under water

What better way to live then by your own rules

No one has written a guideline for life

Because every life is different

And the only one who can tell you what to do

Is the one who is living it

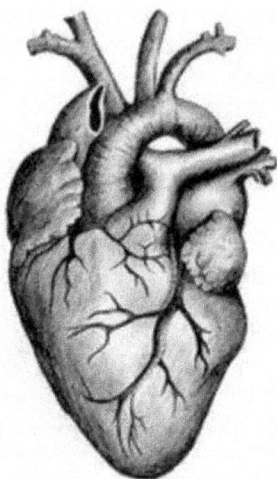

LOVE

Smile at me

Stare in my eyes

Tell me you love me

Hold me when I cry

Make me feel love

Show me passion

Take deep breaths and put your words

In action

Comfort me

Stay for hours

I love you so much

This love will never get sour

Show me a good time

Be yourself

Baby don't worry I want no one else

You are a grateful person
One to remember
When I hear your name
I smile
For I know you bring me joy
Just to hear you say "I love you"
Or open your arms and hug me tight
Makes me love you more
You are my one and only
The one I adore

You are my one and only

I can't forget

The way you hold me

How we met

You hug me tight through all the stress

You keep me close

Through all the mess

Stay with me forever

There won't be any regrets

Show me passion

Show me love

Give me a reason not to give up

Be my forever, be my man

Be the person no one else can

I want to be cherished

From my head to my toes

Got a heart full of gold

A mind full of unspoken treasures

That need to be told

I got that loving

That helps you find your soul

Your love makes me happy
Your love makes me sad
It makes me give thanks
For what I have
It makes me cry
It makes me scream
It makes me laugh
It makes me forget things
It makes me stupid
Stupid in love
For all I ask
Say it again
And this time
Tell me the truth
Do you love me?
Because I love you

There're different kinds of love
Because there's different kinds of people
love defines us
It's what we have inside
It's our strength
And our weakness
It divides us and brings us together
It's all in the mind

My mind is stuck on you

I'm out of breath

And I feel blue

You're in my thoughts

Deep in them too

You caught my eyes

Now I can't get enough of you

Boys

They say they love you with all their hearts

And show their sweet parts

But they don't know

We don't care

And we're sweet everywhere

He makes me smile

He makes me laugh

He makes me want to be his other half

He shows me love

He gives me power

I want him to be mine

For more than a few hours

I want to be your diary

I want you to put your pride in me

I'll show you that I care

As long as you're kind to me

Times get hard

And sometimes even harder

But it's up to us to make this work

No bullshit, No problems

Baby just be honest

We going to make this work

Toss out all your insecurities

You'll be safe with me

Let's run together

Towards our dreams

And make them into our reality

How can I tell you?

I'm so confused

Infatuated with your love

But wanting a new you

There's someone else I see

That you can be

A better you is what I need

I feel a feeling I can't explain
It's like we're going down
But I'm still on top
It's like I want your loving
Not a little but a lot
It's like I want us
But at the same time
Stuck in my thoughts

Jermaine
As I watch you grow

I would've never pictured me

Bringing you home

I would have never expected you in my arms

Yet your love fulfills my soul and heart

My tears flow

And I'm so confused

My heart hurts

Because I want you

Love is crazy in so many ways

But I'm willing to take it on

If you promise to stay

It's been sometime
Since I've felt our chemistry
But I'm still here
Waiting for you to remember me
The reasons we fell in love
The happiness we had
All the times we never gave up

Love me hard

Don't ever give up

I want you to go deep

Deep into my soul

I want that loving

You could never forget

The loving that leaves

Kisses all over my neck

Down my spine

On my behind

Loving me is the

Best thing you could ever find

The love for money
The love for fame
The need to want others
To know your name
It won't get you very far
Just caught up in a game
Where attention is
The goal they seek
Competing for lust
Not knowing the difference
Between it and love

You know that love you crave

That's not a crave for someone else

It's a crave for yourself

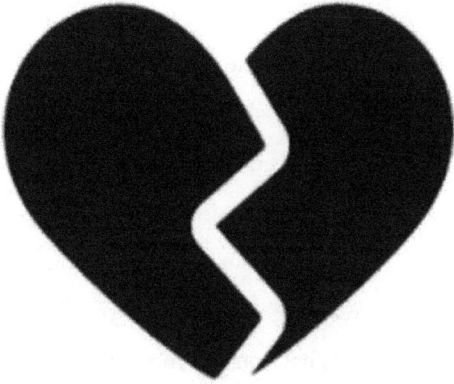

HEARTBREAK

Some would say

They don't wish their pain on to anyone

Not even their worst enemy

So, am I evil?

For wishing mine on to you

Wanting to know that you feel

What you put me through

Every tear, every heartbreak

Every doubt about yourself

It all comes to light

When you're let down

By the one you love

Talking to me with your demands

Only if you knew the things going on in my head

Every word you speak

Seems like it's spoken to offend me

All up in your feelings

Drowning in them

So now you can't see

Can't see the reasons you befriend me

Can't see the reasons why you love me

So now you're stuck

Stuck talking to me with your demands

But only if you knew the things going on in my head

I could never trust a soul

You did it boy

You turned me cold

Lost in a world

That is not my own

Trying to make sense

Of what's going on

You turned me cold boy

Hurt me down to my soul boy

Forgiveness

Is something I had to learn first hand

It ate me alive

I resented him

But it was not only his fault

It was also mine

I blame him

As if I haven't lied

I hurt my heart to keep him there

It's like falling in love with poison

That taste as sweet as the love we first shared

Hearts and kisses don't mean a thing
Blood and bruises reveal the pain
The love that you have isn't the same
The love that you're showing
Isn't a thing
I knew you loved me back then
But now it seems like we're just friends
You made a promise you said you'll keep
You broke a promise
It hurt me
Stay away I don't want you close
My heart is no longer your home

Speaking my feelings is hard to do

Specially around you

You get so mad at first

Then it's me right after you

You leave me so confused

Not knowing if what you say is true

Do you really hate me?

And regret the things you do

Every argument feels like it's deja vu

Every argument the same words are spoken

Does it mean these are your true feelings

I have awoken

All I want is for you to care
Care for me and my feelings
Care for me and my thoughts
Care like how you use to
Way before any of our loss

Lies after lies

How do I survive

Wanting to strive

To be the best of me

Is how I want to live

But it's hard when you can't forgive

Stuck under you not knowing what's the truth

Trying to figure out if what you're telling me is fu

Trying to understand what you're really trying to do

Wondering if you know

God is watching too

And I'm not trying to scare you

Or tell you what to do

I'm just trying to make sure I'm not looking like a fool

I want to be loved the right way

All I ask is for it to come from you

Am I wrong for the feelings I feel

Or are you wrong because you caused me to feel this way

Should I speak on what I'm feeling?

Or stay quiet and heal my own pain

Do you care if I'm not happy?

Cause that's the look that's on your face

How do I escape

Escape the pain

The hurt all the shit you caused me to sustain

I want it all gone

Like the kisses we use to share

What's the point of love

If it's going to feel this way

What's the point of us

If you never mean what you say

Dreams are hard to reach

When there is so much in the way

I want you to push me

Tell me to go for it

Not hold me back

And tell me to wait

I want us both on top

Me and you against the hate

Why wouldn't you want me to succeed

Why wouldn't you want me to be me

I keep count

And seek out

Your intentions

Your thoughts

And try to understand

Why you keep breaking my heart

And it never seems to matter

If I understand or not

Because I'm weak for your love

And tend to forget your faults

Sometimes I wished I was dead

Today you told me you wished the same

What does it mean when pain meets pain

You've brought me into your world

First my love then turned to hate

You taught me a lot about myself

Like how to self-praise

Tell myself I'm beautiful

Cause I know I won't hear it from you

Tell myself to keep smiling, believe, and have faith

The words I always want to hear from you

Those are the words I say

When will it stop
When will I feel powerful next to you
Instead of feeling weak
When will this feeling Seize

I told you she was coming

I warned you

Now stop running

It's time to face the facts

You took a piece of me

I could never get back

You've lied and cheated

Chance after chance

Now look who's heated

Look who's lonely

Look who's scared

I'll sit back

While Ms. Karma gets prepared

We started to lose sight of the love

We had to grab it back

Now it's gone again

And whose fault is that

I've been trying, I swear I am

Now I'm stuck wondering

How to get it back

Why does it seem as if I'm alone?

Where are you

When I need somewhere to call home

If you loved me

It wouldn't be this way

If you care all I see is pain

To tell you the truth

Life's just give and take

Be who you want

I just hope that isn't fake

One day you'll wake up

And I'll be gone

One day you'll wake up

And your love won't be so strong

One day you'll wake up

And I'll wish you the best

Because it will all hurt

Once I've left

We lost sight of the love
And that was the problem
We forgot all about trust
So, there was no us
Left each other lonely
Went and got some new homies
Threw out the respect
And that's what lead us
To broken hearts and shitty regrets

I've seemed to have fallen again

Believed in you

And got let down again

Trying to break a cycle

That has broken me

Trying to repair myself

With self-love

And restore what you stole from me

I tried to convince myself different
Told myself it will get better in a minute
Knowing you were lying wasn't the pain anymore
Lying to myself
That's what's driving me insane
Cause I know better
But I just keep fucking up
Giving you chance after chance
Knowing this isn't love

I have to step away at times

Light a new flame at times

Just to get you out my mind

Wanting a new me with no you

To not be so love sick

Is my dream come true

PERSONAL

She is only 21

With a mind full of dreams

A heart that will never go weak

Her thoughts grew enormous

As if she was a mango tree

Roots so deep under

Branches so high in the sky

Just growing

Through rain and sunshine

I never feel my heartbeat

Never hear a sound

But then I notice

I'm still here

Waiting to be crowned

They take advantage

Of my love, kindness, and pride

It's because of me that they

know the feeling of love

Sometimes I hide for hours straight

To see if you notice

I'm gone away

It feels like your love is nothing

Nothing to cure my pain

To sustain your real ways

It just makes me want to run away

To free my heart from the fear

And be alone again without you my dear

Depression is one hell of a killer
Gun to my father's head
Depression pulled the trigger
11 years old my brother only 9
Grandma brought us the tragedy
December 27th, 2007
"Why lord" my mother cried
Hard to handle
When I haven't seen him in a year
Hard to handle when the last time I got a hug
Was way back to our last visit to him in jail
Hard to handle when my only memories
Are of him being in there
Reminiscing on eating chicken wings
Drinking mango juice, While the guards just stared
Sad that it took his death to bring his family together
He'll always be a part of me
Will always remain my Strength
When I can't find any near

Growing up without a father

I never learned how a man

Should love me

I just took the love I got

Excepted things I should have not

First before I change the world

I must change myself

Little by little

I correct myself

Encourage myself

Better myself

Any way I can

To make sure

I am the best

Myself

I'm learning more and more about myself

The life I live

The people in it

And the ways to live it

I understand all the clichés

And quotes people listen to

I understand how it can comfort you

And put your mind at ease

Help you realize

You're not alone

Someone else feels those feelings too

I wish I could love you

The way I want to

But that will cause me too much pain

Because people never live up to my expectations

And maybe that's my fault

For setting them too high

Or maybe it's their fault

For aiming too low

Now that I think about it

I realized something

Maybe I should choose love over the fear

Instead of combining the two

Maybe I should throw myself

In the deep end once again

Sooner or later I'll learn how to swim

The struggle is real

If you know how it feels

5 kids on your plate

Momma you a queen for real

Bringing in money with your hustle skills

Smiling in our face

But I know your pain isn't healed

I know you want that happiness

They show on tv

Where the families are angels

And act nothing like we

Mama remember you will always be the only woman I see

Remember you will always have my heart too

And when I make it to the top

Just know it's all for you

And when we go through the struggle

Don't worry boo

Because I hate to see it all beat up on you

Don't let it bring you down

Cause it isn't worth it

You got a great heart

Momma in my eyes your perfect

Growing up mixed

I had both ends of the stick

Always asking "oh you black or white?"

No, it goes deeper than that

I'm Jamaican, Italian and Irish

Being around black people

They've always called me white

Still that my hair was nappy

My skin was "too light"

Being around white people

They've always called me black

Still that my skin was light

My hair was "too black"

But I've never needed validation

From no race

Never wanted to be categorized

With no other faces

Because I'm me

And will never define

Myself by society's definitions

And stereotypes

I cannot be put in a box

That would be like believing in

Christopher Columbus and Santa Claus

Sunny days is what I deserve
Then again
The rain is beautiful too
Who am I
To pick between the two
Stormy weather
Is hard to withstand
But once you get through it
It becomes your answer in vain
Constantly reminding myself
My stormy weather
Is what makes me who I am

I sat there staring at them
What if they thought that too
Thought that I could protect them
From every misfortune
What if they thought that too
Sometimes I feel
As if that's something I could do
Lay in the way of the danger
That may come their way
Only to realize
If I want them strong
They must feel pain
They must experience things
For them to learn
They must learn their own way

I never met anyone like her

So open and free

Just living in her sexuality

Her being her

Pushed me to be me

In this book

Is where my soul speaks freely

Where it grows with happiness

Words spilling out of me

Like a jug with no top on it

And it comes so effortlessly

As if I wrote it before

And I'm just rewriting it

They are words straight from my soul

Words that help me

Recognize me, help me become one

A whole

I bet I can get under your skin

Love you from within

Get so deep in your mind

Having conversations no one could begin

Have you so intrigued

Getting you lost in me

Most people want a happily ever after

I want adventures

With limitless dreams

By myself

Alone

on my own

breathe in

breathe out

I'll make it to where my dreams roam

They will become my reality

Quote me word for word

When I say

I am more than the beauty in the eyes of the beholder

I am what they can't see

But can only feel

That agonizing pain

That pleasure that never goes away

Yes this is me

I am very glad to say

Yes this is me

I made me this way

On my own

By myself

All alone

www.ingramcontent.com/pod-product-compliance
Lightning Source LLC
Chambersburg PA
CBHW022206080426
42734CB00006B/568